GLO
What Are Human Rights?

Joseph Harris

FRANKLIN WATTS
LONDON•SYDNEY

First published in 2010 by Franklin Watts

Copyright © 2010 Arcturus Publishing Limited

Franklin Watts
338 Euston Road
London NW1 3BH

Franklin Watts Australia
Level 17/207 Kent Street, Sydney, NSW 2000

Produced by Arcturus Publishing Limited,
26/27 Bickels Yard, 151–153 Bermondsey Street, London SE1 3HA

The right of Joseph Harris to be identified as the author of this work has been asserted by him in accordance with the Copyright, Designs and Patents Act 1988.

Series concept: Alex Woolf
Editor and picture researcher: Jonathan Hilton
Designer: Ian Winton

Picture credits: Corbis: title page (Phillipe Lissac/Godong), 6 (Richard Wainwright), 7 (Bettmann), 8 (Víctor Lerena/epa), 9 (Karoly Arvai/Reuters), 10 (Stapleton Collection), 11 (Lebrecht Music & Arts), 13 top (Richard T Nowitz), 13 bottom (Bettmann), 14 (Bettmann), 15 (Yevgeny Khaldei), 16 (Justin Lane/epa), 17 (Wolfgang Langenstrassen/dpa), 18 (Orban Thierry/Sygma), 19 (Yannis Kontos/Sygma), 21 (Louise Gubb/Saba), 22 (Bettmann), 23 (David Turnley), 24 (Brooks Kraft), 25 (Lacy Atkins/San Francisco Chronicle), 26 (Peter Macdiarmid/epa), 27 (Daniel Deme/epa), 28 (Carlos Cazalis), 29 (George Steinmetz), 30 (Jarekji/Reuters), 31 (Howard Davies), 32 (David Turnley), 33 (JP Laffont/Sygma), 34 (Ali Ali/epa), 35 (Horacio Villalobos/epa), 36 (Arko Datta/Reuters), 37 (Handout/Reuters), 38 (Philippe Lissac/Godong), 40 (Philip Dhil/epa), 41 (S Sabawoon/epa), 42 top (Horacio Villalobos), 42 bottom (Andy Rain/epa).
Getty Images: cover (Paula Bronstein).

Cover caption: A Burmese refugee and his child in the ruins of the refugee camp of Huay Kalok, Thailand, following a flamethrower attack.
Title page caption: In some parts of the world, life is very hard and children like this Egyptian pottery worker have to find full-time jobs.

Every attempt has been made to clear copyright. Should there be any inadvertent omission, please apply to the publisher for rectification.

A CIP catalogue record for this book is available from the British Library.

Dewey Decimal Classification Number: 323

ISBN 978 1 4451 0066 1

Printed in Singapore

Franklin Watts is a division of Hachette Children's Books, an Hachette UK company.
www.hachettelivre.co.uk

SL001356EN

Contents

Chapter 1

What do we mean by human rights?

The idea that there are human rights is a relatively recent one. Since the mid-twentieth century it has become widely accepted that every human being is born with certain rights that cannot be taken away. The idea is based on the belief that we are members of the human family and have the same basic rights, whatever our nationality, sex, colour or religion. Some examples of human rights include the right to life, the right to freedom of speech and the right to a fair trial if you are accused of a crime.

Universal human rights

What makes human rights special is that they are universal: they belong equally to every human being, everywhere in the world. This makes them different from ordinary legal rights, which vary from place to place. Human rights allow for different local laws and customs, but they lay down certain basic rules about how all people should be treated. Making sure that the rules are obeyed is not easy. Almost all countries have accepted human rights in theory. In practice, however, citizens in many countries are likely to be arrested if, for example, they oppose government policies. Unjust government actions of this type are described as human rights violations.

People who have been driven from their homes living in a refugee camp in Chad. Every year millions of people around the world are displaced by wars and natural disasters. They are forced to live in squalid conditions, with inadequate food and very little water.

'We must not be confused about what freedom is. Basic human rights are simple and easily understood: freedom of speech and a free press; freedom of religion and worship; freedom of assembly . . . [and] the right of men to be secure in their homes and free from unreasonable search and seizure and from arbitrary arrest and punishment.'

Eleanor Roosevelt, wife of US president Franklin Delano Roosevelt (1882–1945), expressed her belief in universal human rights in 1948. She was an active campaigner on social issues and served as a delegate to the United Nations

In 1958, Eleanor Roosevelt presented the members of the UN Commission on Human Rights with a publication, *In Your Hands*, celebrating ten years since the proclamation of the Universal Declaration of Human Rights.

Cultural differences

An objection sometimes made to the idea of human rights is that differences in cultural, religious and political beliefs make it impossible to have the same rights everywhere. Countries such as Russia and China sometimes complain that the West uses human rights as an excuse to force its values on the rest of the world. Human rights campaigners argue that human rights do not force people to live in a particular way. Human rights are intended to go beyond cultural differences and to ensure that every person's human dignity and worth is recognized.

National sovereignty

Efforts to enforce human rights often come into conflict with the principle of national sovereignty. A nation's sovereignty means that it is supreme inside its own territory and that its government is therefore free to do as it wishes, without interference. Modern human rights theory holds that a nation's freedom does not extend to violating its citizens' human rights. Yet, in practice, states are often reluctant to interfere with the internal affairs of another country. Today, the international community still struggles to prevent even the most horrific human rights violations.

Balancing rights

Human rights are closely related to the notion of freedom. Rights guarantee freedoms: freedom to live life, make choices and take advantage of opportunities. But the freedoms of individuals or groups may well come into conflict. So, in practice, societies often have to balance freedoms against each other, or even give preference to one person's rights over those of another.

For example, a criminal's right to live in freedom is restricted when he or she is locked up in prison. But this is not a human rights violation because the criminal has violated the rights of others, and the right of the community to live in safety outweighs the criminal's right to freedom. But the situation is not always so clear cut. Does a person's right to drive a gas-guzzling car, for example, outweigh the right of other people to live in a clean environment?

In 2009 activists protested against global warming caused by CO_2 emissions from burning fossil fuels. The right to the benefits of transport and industry can clash with the right to live in a clean environment.

In balancing human rights, the guiding principle is that rights can be limited only when doing so is reasonably justified. A person has the right to listen to loud music, but not if it disturbs other people. Of course, people's ideas about what is 'reasonable' are likely to differ greatly, so there will probably always be disagreements about how to balance rights.

Different types of rights

Human rights are commonly discussed under two headings. One is 'civil and political rights'; the other is 'economic, social and cultural rights'. Broadly speaking, civil and political rights are about the citizen's rights in relation to the state. These rights are intended to prevent the state from oppressing its citizens, and to enable people to live their lives in the way they choose.

Should humans all over the world possess the same basic rights?

Yes

• There are some rights so fundamental that they should be regarded as universal human rights.

• Cultural differences must be respected, but some things are just wrong in any culture.

• Human rights lose all meaning if they do not apply to everybody.

No

• Cultural differences are too great for all societies to be governed by a single set of human rights.

• No one has the authority to decide on a binding list of human rights for the entire planet.

• Some societies emphasize the rights of groups over the rights of individuals. Western ideas of human rights are out of place in such societies.

What's your opinion?

Economic, social and cultural rights seek to ensure that people have a decent standard of living and opportunities to better and fulfil themselves. Both types of rights will be discussed later in the book.

Hungarian riot police are seen here clashing with members of a racist political party in July 2009. This followed a court ruling that outlawed the group on the grounds that it stirred up ethnic tensions. It can be difficult to balance the right to express extremist views with the need to prevent violence.

Chapter 2

How did the idea develop?

Human rights theories are quite a recent development. But some similar ideas appeared in earlier times. For example, some ancient states such as the Roman Republic (509–27 BCE) had laws that limited the rulers' power over their citizens. But not everybody benefited. The laws did not protect everybody, but only citizens. This meant that foreigners and slaves did not have rights. Universal rights were not recognized until the twentieth century.

World religions

All the major world religions suggest that people have rights. In the Jewish Torah, God is said to have given Moses the Ten Commandments. In the sixth Commandment, God told the Jewish people not to kill; to respect the right to life. The Christian messiah, Jesus of Nazareth, taught his followers to love and respect their fellow humans. In Islam, all Muslims were instructed to offer charity to those in need. Ancient Hindu laws state that everyone should be able to live in freedom from violence and poverty. Avoiding violence and showing respect for other living beings is also central to the Buddhist faith.

Religious teachings are not directly concerned with universal human rights. But the existence of similar ideas in religions can encourage different groups to agree on the need for universal human rights.

Magna Carta

Magna Carta, or the 'Great Charter', is an important document in the development of ideas about rights. King John of England (1166–1216) is remembered in popular tales as the villainous enemy of Robin Hood.

A copy of Magna Carta, the document that came to be seen as a basic statement of English liberties. King John was forced to accept it on 15 June 1215 at Runnymede on the River Thames. The king's seal, attached to the document, shows his consent.

King John reigned between 1199 and 1216. He quarrelled with the Church and most of his barons and lost English-ruled territories in France. These failures forced him to agree to the first laws that put limits on the power of the Crown.

The real John was certainly an unpopular ruler. In 1215 the English barons forced him to sign Magna Carta, which set limits on his power. He agreed that in future he would seek the barons' approval before demanding new taxes, and that he would not imprison people without trial.

Magna Carta was not a declaration of human rights. It mainly championed the rights of one group, the barons. But it did establish that the Crown was not above the law, and more and more groups claimed the protection the charter offered. Magna Carta came to be seen as a great statement of English liberties and an important step towards the idea that everyone is equal before the law.

FOCUS

William de Briouze

One of the greatest scandals of King John's reign was his treatment of William de Briouze. In 1208 John claimed that Briouze, Lord of Brecon, owed him money, and he sent a small army to collect it. Briouze fled and John pursued him mercilessly, refusing Briouze's attempts to make peace. Though never tried for any crime, Briouze died in exile in France in 1211. John also put Briouze's wife and eldest son in prison. They were never freed and were probably starved to death. Magna Carta was later forced on John to protect his subjects from such abuses of their rights.

The philosophy of rights: Jean-Jacques Rousseau

For centuries most countries were ruled by kings and queens who were believed to have a god-given right to hold power. But during the seventeenth and eighteenth centuries, political thinkers began to question the relationship between rulers and the people they ruled.

Most of the thinkers imagined that human beings had once lived in a 'natural' state, without society or rulers. If that was so, at some point people must have realized that it would be safer and more pleasant to live in an organized society. When that happened, the thinkers supposed that people made a contract with their future rulers, setting out the terms on which they would govern. The English philosopher John Locke (1632–1704) came to the revolutionary conclusion that if a king abused his subjects, he broke the contract and could be removed.

The Swiss-born French political philosopher Jean-Jacques Rousseau (1712–78) famously wrote that 'Man is born free; yet everywhere he is in chains'. The idea that freedom is natural is very close to the idea of human rights. In his book *The Social Contract* (1762) Rousseau tried to imagine a political system in which human beings could live together without giving up their freedom.

He concluded that societies should be small enough for every citizen to be able to take part in the decision-making process.

Expert View

'The problem is to find a form of association [a community] which will defend and protect with the whole common force the person and goods of each associate [citizen], and in which each, while uniting himself with all, may still obey himself alone, and remain as free as before.'

Jean-Jacques Rousseau expressing his belief in the need for a form of government that safeguards freedom for everyone

The philosophy of rights: Thomas Paine

Thomas Paine (1737–1809) was an English political rebel who went to live in America. In his book *The Rights of Man* (1791) Paine argued that governments must respect the natural rights of man. He took part in the revolutionary movement in the American colonies that led to the Declaration of Independence in 1776.

The American Declaration of Independence on display at the Virginia home of one of the leaders who signed it – Benjamin Harrison. Although the Declaration stated that all men are created equal, estates such as Harrison's were worked by slaves.

The declaration stated that 'all men are created equal; that they are endowed by their Creator with certain unalienable rights; that among these are life, liberty, and the pursuit of happiness'.

These events were still based on a limited idea of freedom. For example, women and slaves did not enjoy equal rights in the new America. But the ideas of eighteenth-century thinkers led on to the philosophy of human rights. In thinking about humanity as a single family and demanding that government be conducted in the interests of the people, Paine expressed ideas that would stand the test of time.

Around 1914 a woman marches along New York's Fifth Avenue during a demonstration in favour of giving women the right to vote. The Declaration of Independence promised men equal rights, but, as in other Western countries, women did not achieve equal rights until the twentieth century.

War crimes

In 1863 Swiss-born Jean Henri Dunant (1828–1910) founded the International Committee of the Red Cross (ICRC) to look after people wounded in wars. The following year the Red Cross produced the first of the treaties known as the Geneva Conventions. These were a set of rules that laid down how soldiers, sailors and prisoners of war should be treated during wartime. Over time, more and more countries agreed to abide by the rules of the treaty. The

This photograph shows Jean Henri Dunant, founder of the Red Cross. He was inspired to create a humanitarian organization after personally witnessing the suffering caused by war. Dunant was one of the winners of the first Nobel Peace Prize in 1901.

FORUM

To what extent had the idea of human rights developed before World War II?

The idea had developed in very important ways:

• The idea of respecting other people's lives and property goes back thousands of years, to ancient societies and religious writings.

• In law, the rights of increasingly large groups were recognized.

• Restrictions on the ill-treatment of wartime enemies suggest an increasing recognition of human dignity and worth.

The idea had not really appeared yet:

• The key to *human* rights is that they apply to all humans.

• Women were not able to vote even in America after the revolution, and slavery continued.

• War crimes against enemy soldiers were illegal, but governments could do whatever they liked to their own people.

What's your opinion?

Conventions now have the status of 'customary international law', which means that all states are bound by them – even those that have not signed the treaty.

The Geneva Conventions forbid combatants to torture or kill enemy prisoners. They also state that wounded prisoners of war must be given medical care. Breaches of the Geneva Conventions are war crimes and can be prosecuted under international law.

The Holocaust

During World War II (1939–45) Nazi Germany conquered much of Europe and murdered citizens of many countries, including Germany. The killings included the mass extermination of 6 million Jews, known as the Holocaust. The trials of Nazi leaders after the war at the Nuremberg tribunals for 'crimes against humanity' were a key moment in the development of human rights. In the past, the Geneva Conventions had forbidden war crimes against combatants, but there was no law or treaty to protect civilians.

The Nuremberg tribunals established the principle that governments could not hide behind their national sovereignty when they committed the wholesale murder of ethnic or religious groups. Such acts, often called ethnic cleansing, are now recognized as the international crime of genocide. A new Geneva Convention was produced in 1949 that forbade wartime mistreatment of civilians as well as military personnel.

Outrage at the crimes committed during the war led governments to try to agree on a set of basic human rights. The modern idea of human rights as rights belonging equally to every human being originated in this period of the twentieth century.

The Nuremberg tribunals of 1945-6, at which leading Nazis were tried for war crimes, carrying out wars of aggression and crimes against humanity. Many of the accused were sentenced to death or given long prison terms.

Chapter 3

How are human rights protected?

Today, most countries accept the idea of human rights, and many rights are protected by international treaties. After World War II new institutions were set up, including the United Nations (UN), and new international laws were introduced. Nazis and Japanese were tried for war crimes. Protecting human rights effectively became an important issue.

The United Nations

In 1945 a total of 51 countries set up the United Nations, an organization in which they could discuss issues and try to overcome conflicts. The protection of human rights was one of the UN's central aims. The Charter of the United Nations declares its intention 'to reaffirm faith in fundamental human rights, in the dignity and worth of the human person, [and] in the equal rights of men and women'.

In 1948 the UN adopted the Universal Declaration of Human Rights (UDHR). This is the basic document of the modern human rights movement. As its name suggests, the UDHR is intended to apply to everyone. This sets it apart from earlier laws, bills of rights and constitutions.

The United Nations today has a total of

Secretary-General of the United Nations Ban Ki-moon addresses the General Assembly in 2008. The Assembly has grown to include almost every country in the world.

A memorial to the victims of the 1994 genocide in Rwanda – a massacre lasting 100 days. The international community was slow to recognize that a genocide was taking place and to respond to the crisis.

192 member states, each with a representative at the UN General Assembly, where members debate global issues and vote on resolutions to express world opinion.

The most important decisions are made by the UN Security Council – a group of five permanent national representatives (USA, UK, France, China and Russia) and ten representatives elected by the General Assembly to serve terms of two years.

Soon after its foundation, the UN established a Commission on Human Rights, and in 2006 a new Human Rights Council replaced the Commission.

The courts

In the 1990s, for the first time since the World War II war crimes trials, the UN set up special courts to try crimes against humanity. The crimes were committed during a war in the Balkans (former Yugoslavia) and during a civil war in Rwanda, Africa.

Then in 2002 the International Criminal Court (ICC) was established, with powers to try cases of genocide, crimes against humanity and war crimes. However, the ICC can try an offence only if a country is involved that accepts the court's jurisdiction. The ICC hopes to protect people worldwide, but many countries dislike the idea of any foreign court putting their own citizens on trial. The establishment of the ICC was opposed by many countries, including the United States, China and Russia.

FOCUS

Genocide conviction

In 1998 Jean-Paul Akayesu became the first person to be convicted of genocide since the Convention on the Prevention and Punishment of the Crime of Genocide was adopted by the UN in 1948. Akayesu was mayor of Taba in Rwanda in 1994 when the Hutu group slaughtered members of the Tutsi minority. Akayesu was found guilty of encouraging the genocide and is serving a life sentence in prison.

NGOs and the media

Non-governmental organizations (NGOs) are organizations that are independent and have no links with any government. Many NGOs have been set up by groups of citizens to campaign on issues such as the environment or human rights. Groups such as Amnesty International and Human Rights Watch raise awareness of the issues and put pressure on governments to end abuses. Because NGOs are independent, they do not have to worry about national interests and can campaign fearlessly.

NGOs can use the media, including film, television, radio and newspapers, to get their message across to the public. Journalists can also draw attention to overlooked human rights crises through investigative reporting.

This demonstrator is a member of an NGO, one of many non-governmental organizations that take advantage of the right to protest. The SOS ('help!') on the 'tree hat' is intended to show that action is desperately needed to save the planet.

International action

Sometimes, countries do take hostile action against another country in an attempt to stop it violating its citizens' human rights. This may take the form of economic sanctions (restrictions on trade) or sometimes even the use of military force.

A serious disadvantage of both measures, however, is that they can hurt the people they are aiming to help. Sanctions can impoverish ordinary people, and military action can cause great damage and the loss of innocent lives.

Governments are strongly influenced by their own national interests, so they are often unwilling to condemn human rights abuses by their allies, or to intervene in parts of the world where they have no special interests. Some observers suspect that the international community was slow to react to the Rwandan massacre in 1994 because it was taking place in an 'unimportant' African country.

Are trade sanctions and military action good ways of pressuring a country with a poor human rights record?

Yes

• When a government is behaving inhumanely, there is sometimes no alternative to strong action.

• Careful planning can minimize the harm done to innocent civilians. Trade sanctions can be applied without cutting off food and medical supplies, and weapons technologies can pick out military targets with great accuracy.

• Even if strong action causes some harm, its success will improve the situation in the long run.

No

• Sanctions and military action risk isolating and impoverishing the target country.

• It would be better to help that country to appreciate the social and economic benefits of living in a free society.

• Strong action may anger the people of the country and cause them to support aggressive policies or terrorism.

What's your opinion?

Despite the problems and dangers involved, there may be times when the international community judges that there is no alternative but to take action against a rights-abusing regime, but this is always likely to be a controversial decision.

Médecins Sans Frontières (Doctors Without Borders) is a humanitarian organization that aims to provide medical care to those who need it most. It was founded in 1971 and was awarded the Nobel Peace Prize in 1999.

Chapter 4

What are civil and political rights?

Civil and political rights are about human beings as citizens and members of the community. They are intended to guarantee freedom, equality, security and the right to have a say in how society is run. They have become part of international law through the International Covenant on Civil and Political Rights. They are sometimes described as 'negative' rights. This is because they order governments *not* to do certain things, such as imprison citizens without trial or torture them.

Equal rights

The Universal Declaration of Human Rights states that all people are equal in rights and dignity, whatever their race, sex, religion or political beliefs. The idea that all people are equal is at the heart of human rights.

FOCUS

The girl of Qatif

In 2006 a 19-year-old girl from Qatif, Saudi Arabia, was dragged out of a male friend's car and raped by seven men. At the trial, the rapists were found guilty and sentenced to time in jail and lashes with a whip. But many people, including many Saudis, were horrified to learn that the rape victim was also sentenced to be lashed. Her crime was being in the company of a man to whom she was not related. In Saudi Arabia it is illegal for women to go out without a male relative to escort them.

Women's rights

During the first half of the twentieth century women's rights improved greatly in the Western world. In 1893 New Zealand became the first country to allow women to vote in national elections. Other countries followed, including the UK (1918) and the USA (1920). New laws increasingly protected women's access to education and jobs.

Today, women in these countries have the same rights as men, although they are still sometimes paid less than male colleagues doing the same work. There is also an ongoing struggle to stop the violence against women that occurs in some homes.

Women in traditional cultures

In some parts of the world, the situation is very different. Women in many countries have few choices about how to live their lives. Many traditional cultures still regard women as inferior to men.

In certain countries, particularly in Africa, girls and young women are subjected to horrific ritual operations on their sexual organs. This practice is called female genital mutilation. The operations are often performed without an anaesthetic and can have serious side effects, such as infection. More than 130 million women have suffered in this way. Various NGOs try to change traditional ways of thinking through education.

However, women as well as men from traditional societies often resist change and wish to hold on to their customs. Some people argue that such attitudes should be respected. Others believe that human rights are so fundamental that cultures and practices that violate them are wrong, and need to change.

These teenagers from the village of Kapchorwa, in eastern Uganda, bravely refused to undergo the genital mutilation ritual that traditionally marks the beginning of adult life among their people. Campaigns to discourage the practice have met with mixed success.

Racial equality

The 1948 Universal Declaration of Human Rights guaranteed equal rights to all ethnic minorities. But this did not make equal rights for minorities a reality. In fact, this was only one step forward in a long struggle.

For most of history, people believed that some races were superior to others. The American Declaration of Independence asserted that 'all men are created equal', but this was not intended to include the black slave population.

Even after the abolition of slavery in the USA in 1865, black people did not yet enjoy equal rights. In the Southern states, laws frequently discriminated against black people, preventing them from using the same facilities as whites. This practice is known as segregation. In the state of Alabama, black people on buses were expected to give up their seats to whites. Things began to change in 1955 when a black woman named Rosa Parks refused to give her seat to a white man. This act of civil disobedience (non-violent refusal to obey unjust laws) has become famous.

Civil rights

In the USA a civil rights movement, which demanded equality before the law, developed in the 1950s and 1960s. But there was fierce resistance to change. Protests sometimes led to violent clashes between demonstrators and police. The most prominent leader of the civil rights movement, the Reverend Martin Luther King, was himself assassinated in 1968.

US police officers and National Guardsmen out in force during the Newark, New Jersey, riots of 1967. The black community – the majority in the city – resented their unfair treatment, and this led to six days of violence in which 26 people died.

FOCUS

Death in Soweto

On 16 June 1976, 12-year-old Hector Pieterson was shot dead by police while protesting against racist education policies in Soweto, South Africa. In South Africa, political power and wealth were concentrated in the hands of whites. The government had a policy of apartheid, which means 'separateness'. Black people were not allowed to vote and received separate, but inadequate, public services (including education and health care). The killing of Hector Pieterson was just one example of the brutality of the apartheid era, which came to an end when fully democratic elections were held in 1994.

Hector Pieterson's mother prays at his graveside. His killing during the Soweto riots became a symbol of the brutality of the apartheid regime. The day of Hector's death, 16 June, is now commemorated as South Africa's National Youth Day.

But by then the protest movement itself had largely succeeded. The USA has made vigorous efforts to end discrimination on the basis of race. Many see the election in 2008 of the first black president, Barack Obama, as a symbol of the progress made.

Freedom

Civil and political rights guarantee certain freedoms and protections. The most fundamental is the right to live in freedom itself. Many people all over the world are not fully free. The completely unfree – slaves – are even worse off. Slaves are treated as the property of their 'owners'. Slavery is recognized as an international crime. But it still exists, and so does human trafficking (the selling of human beings). Poor families in Africa sometimes sell their children into slavery in order to survive. One of the most common forms of human trafficking is to force women to become prostitutes.

Crime and punishment

Sometimes there are good reasons to restrict a person's freedom, as in the case of people who break the law. But punishments, even for criminals, must be in line with the standards laid down in human rights law. For example, people must not be detained (held against their will) without just cause, they must receive a fair trial if they are accused of a crime and they must be regarded as innocent until proved guilty.

Torture

A number of international treaties absolutely forbid the use of torture. The human rights movement believes that torture – like genocide and slavery – is an international crime and can never, no matter what the circumstances, be justified. However, many undemocratic regimes around the world, including China, have continued to use torture despite international protests.

FOCUS

Detained without trial

In late 2001 Murat Kurnaz was arrested while travelling in Pakistan and transferred to the US detention camp in Guantánamo Bay, Cuba. He was held there for five years without being tried or convicted of a crime. According to his account, he was beaten, tortured with electric shocks to the feet, hung for hours by his arms and forced to inhale water. Released documents suggest that Kurnaz had quickly been cleared of suspicion of links with terrorism. But he was nonetheless kept in captivity until 2006.

Soldiers lead a prisoner through the US base at Guantánamo Bay, Cuba. The base is used to hold suspects seized during the US 'war on terror'. NGOs have campaigned against alleged human rights abuses at the camp.

This 2009 protest in San Francisco is against the use of torture by the USA on terror suspects. The protestors are acting out the humiliation and ill treatment of prisoners, including waterboarding, in which the victim is made to breathe in water to simulate being drowned.

In democracies, there have recently been arguments about how much pressure can be put on suspects during questioning before 'pressure' really becomes just another word for torture. The increase in terrorist attacks, such as the assault on the USA on 11 September 2001, when the twin towers of the World Trade Center in New York City were destroyed and thousands of people died, made many people feel that tougher questioning of terrorist suspects might be justified.

Human rights activists believe that a civilized society cannot permit torture in any circumstances, and cannot brutalize its citizens by training them to inflict pain on others. They also argue that torture is not a reliable way of extracting information, and that if torture were allowed some innocent people would inevitably suffer by mistake.

Crossing the line?

In 2007 the media broke the story that the American CIA (Central Intelligence Agency) had secretly been using a technique known as 'waterboarding', in which victims are forced to breathe in water so that they feel as though they are drowning. Some people were horrified. Others felt that the terrorist threat justified such extreme measures. When US president Barack Obama took office in January 2009 he banned waterboarding, stating that the technique violated American ideals and values.

The right to life

Society has an obligation to protect the lives of its members. But even the right to life raises questions. Should society be able to kill people as a form of punishment? When is it acceptable to kill someone in order to protect others?

The death penalty

In many countries, the state may put people to death – usually for committing serious offences, such as murder. According to Amnesty International, in 2008 three states – China, Iran and Saudi Arabia – accounted for 90 per cent of the world's executions. Together, they put to death at least 2,166 people. Organizations such as

FOCUS

Living on death row

In the USA, Troy Davis was convicted of killing a police officer and was sentenced to death in 1991. He has been trying to appeal against his conviction ever since. Several of the prosecution witnesses have since changed their stories, claiming that they were pressured by the police to implicate Davis. Serious doubts have been expressed about the truthfulness of another two witnesses. But the courts refused to hear the new evidence until August 2009, when the US Supreme Court stepped in. If Davis is declared innocent at the retrial, his life will no longer be in danger. But there is no doubt that in countries that still retain the death penalty the innocent sometimes suffer the ultimate penalty.

A bus destroyed by a bomb during the terror attacks on the London transport system on 7 July 2005. More than 700 people were injured and 52 were killed. Some people argue that certain human rights will have to be sacrificed in order to fight and defeat terrorism.

Amnesty International argue that the death penalty violates the right to life. At present there is no international agreement on this issue, although in 2007 the UN General Assembly passed a resolution calling for a halt to the death penalty. Human rights activists are encouraged by declining execution rates in some places. The United States executed 37 people in 2008, the lowest yearly rate since 1995.

Killing in self-defence

Sometimes police officers are forced to kill in order to protect themselves and others. But these cases are not always clear cut. Law-enforcement officers are clearly justified in shooting someone who is pointing a gun at them, but what if the officers think there is a gun, but it is dark and hard to be certain? Should they hesitate and risk their own lives and those of other people nearby? What if they fear that the suspect may be about to detonate a bomb?

A tragic example of this was the killing of a young Brazilian man, Jean Charles de Menezes. He was shot dead by police on a train at an underground station in London, England, on 22 July 2005. The officers wrongly believed that he was one of four suicide bombers whose plot to murder underground train passengers had been foiled the day

Members of Jean Charles de Menezes' family hold a press conference as part of their 'Justice for Jean' campaign. The family took legal action against the police for the killing of de Menezes in London. In November 2009 the police agreed to pay compensation.

before. Two weeks earlier, suicide attacks had claimed the lives of 52 London commuters. In these circumstances, the police were afraid that, if challenged, the man might immediately detonate a bomb, so they killed him at once. As a result, an innocent man died. But what if the police hesitate in future, giving a suspect time to detonate a bomb? There are no easy answers to these questions.

Freedom of association and assembly

The freedom of association and of assembly are crucial rights. They ensure that people can form groups – political parties or trade unions, for example – to promote their interests or views, and can meet and protest freely.

Trade unions

Trade unions are organizations formed by workers who hope to improve their pay and conditions by acting together. Individual workers generally find it difficult to oppose the decisions of their managers or bosses. But in a trade union, workers can be helped by skilled negotiators and can use the threat of withdrawing their labour (a strike) in order to improve their bargaining position. Dictatorships have often banned trade unions and severely limited the right of people to associate freely.

Protest

In a free society, people can assemble to protest or to demand remedies for their grievances. Provided that they act non-violently, they are even free to oppose all the policies of their government. Some governments, however, do not tolerate dissent (disagreement). In 2009 the Iranian government cracked down hard on protestors who claimed that the result of the June presidential elections was fraudulent. Dozens of protesters were killed and hundreds more arrested.

Supporters of the reformist presidential candidate Mir-Hossein Mousavi are seen here protesting against the 2009 election results in Tehran, Iran. The protestors claimed that the election was fixed in favour of the conservative president Mahmoud Ahmadinejad.

Banks of CCTV screens in the Joint Operations Command Center in the US capital, Washington, DC. This high-tech centre allows the authorities to monitor activities throughout the entire city.

In the early twenty-first century the terrorist threat led some democratic governments to increase restrictions on protest. Governments feared that terrorists might exploit protests or use them as a cover for their activities. In the UK the police were given extra powers to restrict the size and location of protests. In an effort to learn about terrorists' plans, the security services were given increased powers to hear or read personal communications, such as phone calls or emails. Some people argue that these restrictions on rights are necessary to keep society safe. Others, however, believe that such chipping away at human rights is a dangerous development.

FOCUS

Tank man

The 'tank man' was an unidentified protestor who took part in demonstrations in China between April and June 1989. Thousands of Chinese gathered in Beijing in and around Tiananmen Square. Many different groups were involved, but most were calling for greater freedom and a say in how the country was run. In June the government decided to halt the protests and sent in the army. Many people were killed – the casualties numbered in the thousands according to Western journalists. The tank man stood defiantly in the way of a column of tanks as they tried to drive into the square. His image was captured by photographers and became famous around the world.

Freedom of speech

The right to freedom of speech allows people to exchange ideas without being punished. In some countries newspapers are controlled by the government and are used to promote its policies. In nations with free speech, the media can report the truth as it sees it, making it more difficult for governments to abuse their power.

Even in a free society there are limits on freedom of speech, especially where it would interfere with other people's freedoms. Publishing lies or unproven statements is illegal and is called libel. When the offending words are spoken, the crime is called slander.

Freedom includes the freedom to hold and express ideas that most people regard as repulsive. But limits are imposed on free speech when the ideas expressed could be harmful. In free societies, people are not imprisoned for having racist opinions, but there are laws against inciting racial hatred.

Freedom of religion is a human right, but religious groups sometimes find it hard to accept freedom of speech from critics. In 2004 *Behzti*, a play by a Sikh woman author, was staged in Birmingham, UK. Its scenes of violence and sexual abuse, set inside a Sikh temple, deeply offended some Sikhs. Violent protests forced the theatre to cancel the play.

Some people believe that there should be limits on free expression when it is insulting to religious groups. An alternative view is that, in a free society, it should be possible to offend everyone equally.

Jordanian Muslims burn flags in their protest against cartoons of Muhammad published in a Danish newspaper in 2005 and, later, in other countries as well.

Asylum

Human rights law guarantees everyone the right to escape persecution in their own country and to seek asylum elsewhere. But asylum seekers may well arrive without money and do not always speak the local language. There is often a suspicion that

FORUM

Should the use of torture be absolutely forbidden?

Yes

• Torture is a barbaric practice that cannot be tolerated under any circumstances.

• Innocent people may be tortured by mistake.

• The information extracted from people under tortured may not be reliable.

No

• Some threats must be stopped by any means – for example, a planned terrorist attack using a nuclear weapon.

• We should protect law-abiding people rather than criminals and terrorists.

• The right not to be tortured should be weighed against the right to life of victims of terror.

What's your opinion?

asylum seekers are just pretending to be refugees in order to get into a country where they will be better off financially. However, studies have shown that most asylum seekers who seek entry to the UK are trying to escape real dangers.

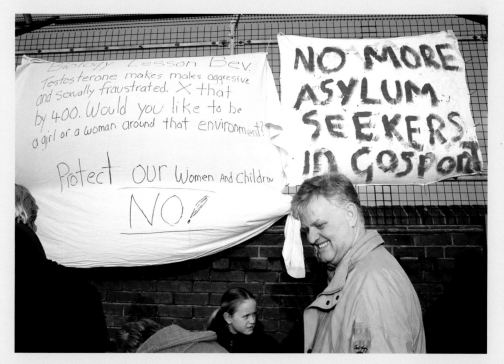

In this protest in Gosport, England, in 2002, thousands of local residents demonstrated against plans to house 400 asylum seekers locally. The plans were finally abandoned by the authorities. Finding suitable places to house asylum seekers raises great difficulties.

Chapter 5

What are economic, social and cultural rights?

Economic, social and cultural rights aim to guarantee everyone a basic standard of living and educational and health benefits. They are protected by the International Covenant on Economic, Social and Cultural Rights. Rights of this kind are sometimes described as being 'positive' rights, because they require the government to take action to ensure that benefits – such as enough food and water, adequate housing and health care and the chance to work for a living – are available.

Criticism

Opponents of economic, social and cultural rights argue that human rights are about securing people's ability to live freely. They believe that classifying food and health care as rights interferes with the freedom of governments to make their own decisions. And governments will probably have to limit other rights and freedoms in order to provide social, economic and cultural ones. In order to provide health care for the poor, for example, a government has to take money (in the form of taxes) from its better-off citizens.

Human rights campaigners argue that all rights are connected. Economic, social and cultural rights serve as a reminder that society must protect the interests of all of its members, and not just the privileged or even the majority. Without these rights, the disadvantaged in society will never have the wealth or education to enjoy the freedoms guaranteed by their civil and political rights.

These Somali children are starving. Many of the world's people do not have enough food and water to sustain life. Even so, not everyone agrees that access to food and water should be a human right.

Food and water

People need access to food and clean drinking water in order to survive. In many parts of the world these are not available. Arguably, civil and political rights, such as the right to freedom of speech, mean very little to people if their basic needs are not being met and they are struggling just to survive.

The idea behind the right to food and the right to water is not that the government should provide them free to all, but that everyone should be able to access them. Governments should make sure that no one is evicted from their farmland or denied access to food because they belong to a minority group. Governments should also provide for emergency food in case of shortages, and should have social security arrangements to help the unemployed, the disabled and other disadvantaged citizens.

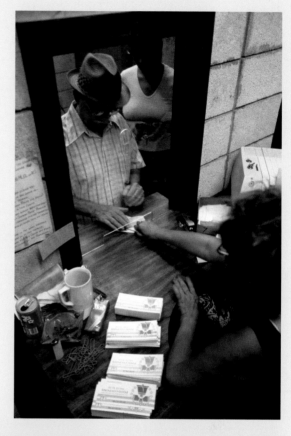

This man is receiving food stamps in Miami, Florida. Wealthy nations such as the USA have systems in which the government provides money or free food so that the poorest do not starve.

FOCUS

The price of water

In 2000 the Bolivian government sold the city of Cochabamba's water system to a group of Western corporations. Soon after the corporations took over, the cost of water rose steeply. Mother-of-four Tanya Paredes became a symbol of the injustice. Her water bill tripled, costing her more than three times the amount needed to feed her family for a week. After strong popular protests, the water system was returned to government control. The right to food and water does not mean that water utilities must be publicly owned. But it does mean that water companies, public or private, must provide water at prices that everyone can afford.

Housing

Another basic human need is shelter. The right to housing implies that everyone should have access to decent, clean accommodation, washing facilities and waste disposal. There is currently a world housing crisis. The UN estimates that 1.6 billion people live in inadequate housing with failures of water supply and sanitation. However, housing problems are not found in poor countries alone. Homelessness is a problem in even the wealthiest of developed nations.

Expert View

What are the responsibilities of an occupying power towards the people under their control during a period of armed conflict?

'Gaza's 1.5 million [Palestinian] people are enduring a serious humanitarian crisis brought on by more than two weeks of major military operations . . . Gaza's civilians are facing dire shortages of food, water, cooking gas, fuel and medical care . . . in some places open sewage is spilling into the streets. Children, who make up 56 per cent of Gaza's residents, are especially vulnerable. Humanitarian law provides that Israel as an occupying power must ensure the safety and well-being of the civilian population. The blockade is a form of collective punishment in violation of international law.'

The Human Rights Watch report, Deprived and Endangered, *describing the human rights crisis in Gaza in 2009*

A Palestinian man shelters in the ruins of his home in the Gaza Strip, following an Israeli strike in January 2009. According to the Israeli army, action was taken in response to a rocket attack launched from Gaza against the Israeli city of Askelon.

Three homeless men living in tents in 2006, but this picture was not taken in a war-torn country – the site is in the prosperous French capital, Paris. The tents, set up along the Canal Saint Martin, were provided by the charity Children of Don Quixote.

Housing during conflict

The right to housing is hard to apply during armed conflicts, when there is often large-scale damage to civilian property as a result of the fighting. Such damage may be inevitable, but intentional, wholesale destruction of housing and forced eviction of people from their homes are crimes under international law.

The issues involved are particularly difficult. During World War II, in a life-and-death struggle, both sides carried out 'saturation bombing' to destroy cities and undermine their enemies' morale. More recently, the conflict between Israel and the Palestinians has also led to the destruction of many Palestinian homes in controversial circumstances. The Israelis are threatened by terrorist attacks, and they claim that the destruction caused by their military responses is unavoidable. Opinions are strongly divided as to whether or not such actions are justified.

Workers' rights

Employment rights protect people from mistreatment at work. Concern with working conditions began earlier than the human rights movement. Workers have banded together in trade unions for hundreds of years. The International Labour Organization (ILO) was founded in 1919 to define international standards and to make sure that workers everywhere were fairly treated. Today, working conditions can be seen as part of human rights.

In societies where human rights are respected, people are not forced to work against their will. In addition, workers are protected against unfair dismissal, they are paid fairly and they are provided with a safe working environment.

In many parts of the world, however, these rights hardly exist. People in poor countries often have no choice, but must work extremely long hours for very little pay. Others are trapped by debt and must work like slaves to meet the payments. In places, women are even kidnapped and forced to become prostitutes.

In 2004, children hold a banner as part of a protest against child labour in Bombay, India. Human rights campaigners argue that children have a right to an education, and should not be forced to work. But child labour is still common in developing countries.

Some countries' economies depend on the ready availability of cheap labour. Conditions and pay are often terrible, and workers who try to form trade unions may be dealt with brutally. Even child labour is still used in some places. Young children spend all day working – for example, sewing items to be sold in Western sporting-goods stores – instead of attending school or going out to play. Nowadays, Western consumers are often angry when they learn that companies are using child labour to manufacture their products. Such people stop buying the goods in order to try to persuade the companies to change their policies.

Rights in the developing world

Reaching agreements on workers' rights can be difficult because some countries are so much poorer than others. Developing countries are often hostile to workers' rights that would lead to increases in pay and improvements in working conditions. This is because a cheap local workforce keeps down costs and is often an incentive for big corporations to set up businesses in developing countries. It has been argued that losing these advantages by introducing new working standards could cost workers their jobs and so leave them worse off than they were before. Human rights advocates argue that this claim is exaggerated. They believe that it is possible to apply minimum standards everywhere without preventing developing countries from attracting investment, since their labour will still be far cheaper than in the developed world.

FOCUS

Union organizer killed

On 10 March 2008 a trade union organizer, Gerardo Cristobal, was murdered in Imus, Philippines. Armed men pursued and shot him while he was driving his car. He had survived a previous attempt on his life in 2006, and he was the second workers' representative at the EMI-Yazaki semiconductor plant to be killed in recent years. Unionists complained that the police did nothing to investigate the crime, and allegations were made that the police were involved in the attack. Union leaders who attempt to stand up for workers' rights have been targeted in many parts of the world.

El Salvador police arrest suspects following the murder of visiting American union organizer José Gilberto Sato. Sato had come to the country to see members of his family and to meet Salvadoran truckers.

Education and health

Economic, social and cultural rights promise everyone the right to education and the right to health. Access to education and health care is vital if people are to develop and live healthy and happy lives.

Access to education

The right to education means that governments must provide free and compulsory primary schooling for all their country's children. They must also do as much as possible to help people to afford secondary and university education. Education must be made available to all children without exception.

Like most human rights, the right to education is not yet satisfactorily enforced everywhere. In many parts of the world, for example, boys receive a better education than girls. Children who work and children who live on the streets seldom receive any schooling.

Primary school children attend class in Senegal, Africa. Senegal's constitution guarantees all children the right to education. But the reality falls short of this. In 2005 an estimated 30% of children aged five to fourteen worked instead of attending school.

Health care

The right to health should guarantee access to health-care treatment. This means that everyone should be able to afford treatment, either through a publicly owned provider (for example, the UK's National Health Service) or through privately purchased health insurance.

HIV/AIDS

Efforts to provide a universal right to health still have a long way to go. In Africa, there is an epidemic of HIV, the virus that develops into an illness called AIDS. AIDS destroys the body's natural defences against infection. Currently, medicines only slow down the progress of the disease. To make matters worse, not enough Africans have access to

Should economic, social and cultural rights be universally enforced?

Yes

• Basic human needs must be satisfied for people to live in a free and equal society.

• Yes, but governments should be free to provide access to food, water, housing, education and health in ways that suit their own societies.

• It is reasonable to insist that governments provide all their citizens with the necessities of life. It should not be within their power to decide not to.

No

• Not all governments have the resources to guarantee these rights, so it is meaningless to call them 'rights'.

• If the conditions in a country make necessities such as food and housing too expensive, granting everyone such 'rights' would work only if somebody else was willing to pay for them – for example, through foreign aid.

• Countries should be left to decide for themselves how to distribute their limited resources.

What's your opinion?

this medicine. In 2005, the G8 – a group of the world's richest nations – pledged to work towards universal availability of the medication by 2010. There has, in fact, been significant progress in providing access to the vital drugs, but the majority of African AIDS sufferers still go untreated.

Access in the developed world

Parts of the developed world also have problems in providing universally accessible health care. The USA, for example, does not have a national health service, paid for out of taxes, so Americans have to pay for their own private health care. The American private system could provide universal health care only if everyone paid for insurance to cover the costs of any treatment they needed. But in reality, many people cannot afford the cost of the insurance or do not choose to have it. In 2009, 46 million people in the USA did not have health insurance. The issue was hotly debated in the country when President Obama announced plans to expand government-run health-care programmes for people who could not afford private treatment.

Chapter 6

Has the human rights movement had an impact?

Human rights have introduced a new way of thinking about issues. Today, any new law, natural disaster or conflict is likely to be discussed in terms of its impact on human rights. There are disagreements over important details, but the basic idea that all humans have the right to be treated with dignity is accepted by most governments. But there is a big difference between what governments say and what they do. States that have ratified (approved) human rights treaties often, in practice, commit human rights violations.

Human rights crises

Humanitarian crises have continued to occur despite the many international human rights treaties produced by the UN. There have been several cases in which the UN and powerful countries have failed to step in to stop the most horrific of all human rights violations – genocide.

A notable example is the struggle that has been going on since 2003 in Darfur in the Sudan. The conflict is between Arab and non-Arab Sudanese. An Arab militia, allegedly backed by the Sudanese government, has carried out mass killings of non-Arab groups. The UN estimates that 300,000 people have died as a result of the conflict. Despite the war crimes being committed in Darfur,

Sudanese President Omar Hassan al-Bashir waves to his supporters at a rally in March 2009. He is wanted by the International Criminal Court for war crimes and crimes against humanity. But he is unlikely to turn himself in.

FOCUS

Victory for international pressure

In 2006 a young student, Sayed Pervez Kambaksh, was arrested and sentenced to death in Afghanistan. His crime was blaspheming against (insulting) Islam by spreading information about women's rights. But when the British newspaper *The Independent* reported on his situation, tremendous pressure was put on the Afghan government by other governments and human rights NGOs. His sentence was first changed to 20 years in prison and then, after continued campaigning, he was set free in September 2009. In this instance, pressure in support of human rights achieved a great result.

Sayed Pervez Kambaksh, seen here during an appeal hearing at a court in Kabul, Afghanistan, in October 2008. His appeal was unsuccessful. But in September 2009, President Hamid Karzai allowed Kambaksh to leave the country.

the UN Security Council decided to send in UN peacekeeping troops only in July 2007. Critics argued that the international response was much too slow. According to the peacekeeping forces in the Sudan, the conflict had finally died down by August 2009.

Enforcing human rights

The enforcement of human rights is difficult. The UN Security Council has the power to take action against a nation that is abusing human rights. But this rarely happens due to the way the Security Council works. Each of the five permanent members has the ability to veto (overrule) any decision. This means that members with bad human rights records are not likely to support action against fellow offenders. China, in particular, has a very poor human rights record and has developed close relationships with other regimes that also violate human rights. Human rights NGOs have accused China of aiding genocide in Darfur by supplying the Sudanese government with weapons.

The 'rights culture'

The current emphasis on rights has provoked opposition among some people, who feel that it has gone too far. They argue that too great a focus on rights leads to exaggerated, demanding attitudes on the part of groups and individuals. Groups such as the disabled and immigrants now demand their rights forcefully, and that can cause resentment. One point of view is that the 'rights culture' should be balanced by an awareness of the duties involved in good citizenship.

French Muslims protest against the government's ban on religious symbols in schools, which prevents girls from wearing the headscarves required by their beliefs.

Nevertheless, protection of the rights of minority groups is an important goal of the human rights movement. For example, immigrants are often targeted because they are 'different', and human rights activists stress that it is important to defend the right of immigrants to follow their own customs and ways of life. However, it has also been argued that more should be done to encourage immigrant minorities to accept and, as far as possible, share the values and customs of the host community.

A better world?

How much of an impact has the human rights movement had? Its failures are clear. Gross violations of human rights still occur all over the world, often unpunished. But

2009 & STILL STRIPPED of our PENSIONS

An extreme case of 'rights culture'? In June 2009, half-naked ('stripped') demonstrators protested outside the Houses of Parliament, in London, UK, against the government's failure to guarantee their lost company pensions.

action to protect human rights has had an effect. In 1999, forces sent by NATO (the North Atlantic Treaty Organization) liberated the province of Kosovo, whose people were struggling to win their independence from Serbia. And although the UN may react slowly, its peacekeepers have been sent all over the world. Human rights laws have led to the conviction of individuals for war crimes. And pressure from NGOs such as Amnesty International has helped to rescue many unjustly condemned people.

The idea of human rights has had tremendous publicity thanks to TV, radio and the newspapers. It is part of most people's thinking and almost all governments accept the idea. Governments that abuse human rights feel they must pretend that they haven't, and deny or offer excuses for what they have done. They may appear to ignore world opinion, but in many cases it has at least some effect on how they behave.

These are real gains, even if they are limited ones. The idea of human rights will not bring about a perfect world in the foreseeable future, but it will almost certainly help to create a better one for most people.

FORUM

Do you think the increasing recognition of universal human rights has improved people's lives?

Yes
- People in many countries are now very aware of human rights. They often donate money to help promote human rights elsewhere or protest against abuses.

- International pressure for human rights makes countries less likely to commit abuses.

- Human rights law has allowed the punishment of people for war crimes.

- Pressure from human rights NGOs has influenced government policies and helped to free unjustly imprisoned people.

No
- Even 60 years on from the Universal Declaration of Human Rights, many countries still ignore human rights.

- Politics is dominated by self-interest. Governments will never put human rights ahead of national interest.

- Human rights are not acceptable in many places because they attempt to impose Western values on other parts of the world.

What's your opinion?

Glossary

AIDS Stands for Acquired Immune Deficiency Syndrome, a deadly disease that destroys the human body's natural defences (immune system) against infection.

Amnesty International A non-governmental organization (NGO) that campaigns to end human rights abuses around the world.

apartheid The policy of racial segregation in South Africa, which ended in 1994.

asylum Refuge that people hope to find from persecution in their own countries.

blockade A situation in which supplies or people are prevented from going in or out of a country.

civil disobedience The non-violent refusal to obey laws that are regarded as oppressive or unjust.

civil rights Rights that guarantee everyone can live safely as a free and equal member of a community.

culture The way of life, customs and beliefs of a group of people.

economy The resources, money and work of a country, or group of countries, and the way in which they are shared out.

ethnic Describes a group with a shared origin or culture.

General Assembly One of the main bodies of the United Nations (UN), organization in which all member states are represented.

Geneva Conventions International treaties that lay down how states should treat enemy soldiers and civilians during a war.

genocide The intentional destruction of an entire ethnic or religious group.

HIV Stands for Human Immunodeficiency Virus, the virus that causes AIDS.

International Criminal Court (ICC) The first permanent international court established to try people for genocide, crimes against humanity and war crimes.

International Labour Organization (ILO) An agency, now part of the UN, that specializes in workers' rights.

international law The body of laws that countries have agreed should apply to them all.

investment Putting money into a business or country. A large corporation might invest in a developing country by building a factory and hiring workers.

Islam The Muslim religion.

Magna Carta The legal document, signed by King John in 1215, that is generally regarded as the basis of English liberties.

media Newspaper, TV, radio, films, websites and similar forms of mass communication.

minority group A group that is different from the majority in a country – for example, for ethnic or religious reasons.

national sovereignty A country's right to run its own internal affairs, without outside interference.

non-governmental organization (NGO) An organization that operates independently of any national government.

North Atlantic Treaty Organization (NATO) A military alliance consisting of the United States and a number of European countries.

persecution Sustained mistreatment of an individual or group, often based on ethnic or religious hatred.

primary school A school for young children that teaches basic skills such as reading, writing and arithmetic.

Red Cross An international movement that looks after the injured, particularly in wartime.

Roman Republic An ancient state centred on the city of Rome, Italy.

Security Council A key body of the UN, with the power to make important decisions, such as authorizing military action.

segregation Keeping different groups separate, usually so that one group is privileged.

Supreme Court, USA The highest court in that country. Its decisions are final.

terrorism Acts of violence carried out to create fear and promote a cause.

Torah The first five books of the Bible that together comprise the most important holy text of Judaism, the Jewish religion.

trade union An organization in which workers act together to protect or improve their wages and conditions.

unalienable An old-fashioned form of the word 'inalienable', describing something – for example, a right – that cannot be taken away.

United Nations (UN) The international organization founded after World War II to promote peace and human rights.

universal Applying equally to everyone.

veto The power to stop a proposed law or action from going into effect, even if it is supported by the majority.

war crimes Actions that violate the laws of war – for example, murdering or enslaving prisoners.

waterboarding A type of torture in which, over and over again, the victims are made to feel as though they are drowning.

Western world A term that describes the wealthy democratic nations, most of which are in western Europe and North America.

Further information

Books

Every Human Has Rights, National Geographic Society, 2008

Holocaust by Simon Adams, Franklin Watts, 2005

Human Rights: who decides? (*Behind the news* series) by Ann Kramer, Heinemann, 2007

The United Nations (*Global Organizations* series) by Sean Connolly, Franklin Watts, 2008

We Are All Born Free: The Universal Declaration of Human Rights in Pictures, Amnesty International, Frances Lincoln Children's Books, 2008

Websites

www.bbc.co.uk/worldservice/people/features/childrensrights/childrenofconflict

A BBC site with information and personal stories about children suffering a range of human rights abuses.

www.humanrightsproject.org/content.php?sec=video

The Human Rights Video Project has a selection of documentary films about human rights.

http://library.thinkquest.org/J0112391

A site about the US civil rights movement, including timeline, leader profiles and games.

www.un.org/cyberschoolbus/humanrights/index.asp

The UN's educational pages on human rights include a plain-language version of the Universal Declaration, along with questions and activities.

Index

Entries in **bold** are for pictures.